AUGUSTA

APRILIA

ARDEA

APPIA

AURELIA

FLAMINIA

LANCIA

Probably one of the prettiest, and certainly one of the grandest, Lancias Farina ever built. This drop-head coupé from the late 1930s, comes from a period when Farina was also experimenting with the slatted fronts brought into fashion by Gordon Buehrig's Cord. In this car however, he opted for the more restrained re-working of the standard Lancia grille, and a noticeable lack of embellishment. The car itself is particularly interesting, in that it was discovered in a poor state not so very long ago; and was completely refurbished by the original coachbuilders. In recent years the car has been owned by Mr. Michael Scott, who has now parted with it; and, at the time of writing, seems likely to end its days in the National Motor Museum at Beaulieu. There could hardly be a more fitting resting place for this, the most British of Italian cars.

LANCIA

Michael Frostick

DALTON WATSON LTD
LONDON

First Published 1976

ISBN 0 901564 222

© Dalton Watson Ltd 1976

Process Engravings by Star Illustration Works Ltd
Printed in England by the Lavenham Press Ltd
for the publishers
DALTON WATSON LTD
76 Wardour Street, London W1V 4AN

Distributed in the U.S.A. by
Motorbooks International
Osceola, Wisconsin 54020

Author's Note

Collectors of this series of "one-make" books hardly need reminding again that this is not a history of the marque. However, Lancia enthusiasts, who may have had no interest in the volumes that have preceeded this, might be glad of the disclaimer. As before, the aim has been to include a picture of as many Lancias as the company's files and diligent research have made available; and while history must pervade the pages, it is a love of motor cars rather than a love of history that have prompted its writing, its collation, and its publication.

From the start Lancia seemed a very well worth-while project. Lancia himself was an innovative engineer in the grand manner, and his lifelong friendship and association with Pinin Farina has meant that more often that not his ideas have worn the most elegant of shapes. The combination of the two minds, of Lancia and Farina, makes both the product and this book unique. That the men who now control Lancia should have been able to pursue the founders ideals, and continue the collaboration with their chosen coachbuilder, is a matter of remark; and makes uncommon sense when seen in the unfolding of these pages.

As is usual with a book of this nature, nothing at all would be possible without the help of the manufacturers themselves; and my first thanks must therefore go to Sandro Fiorio of the Lancia press department, and to Marie-Pierre Baggio who delved endlessly into her newly created filing system to find the answers to all the most difficult questions. Bob Crowther of Lancia in London also comes high on the list for his enthusiasm in the early stages, when the project might otherwise have been still-born, and his constant willingness to help at all times has been very heartening.

Dr. Amaro at the Biscaretti museum pulled some last minute surprises from his files, and Fredi Vallentini at Pininfarina found the answers to some pictures which would otherwise have remained mysteries for ever.

In England, The National Motor Museum was its usual helpful self, and Nick Georgano, its photo librarian, is responsible for the only two racing Lambdas in the book, and the charming shot on Beggar's Roost. The Autocar has provided a number of pictures as usual; and Lawrie Dalton's photographic friends in West London, C. K. Bowers & Sons, have come up with some British bodies that might otherwise have been forgotten. Michael Scott has provided the frontispiece, depicting one of the loveliest Lancias ever. To all these people I am much indebted.

Contents

Vincenzo Lancia - the man

The story of Lancia is, first and foremost, the story of a man. A man of ideas, who had the drive and ability to set himself up in business (in the halcyon days when such things were still possible) to turn the products of his mind into the realities of metal. His name was indelibly stamped on all the models made in his lifetime, as much as those of Bentley or Bugatti; and it is to the great credit of the men who have followed him in the running of the business, that one can feel the same is true to-day. Had Vincenzo Lancia lived on into the seventies it seems likely that he would have been pleased with what Lancia are making now.

The family came from the mountains in the north of Italy; and it is usually said that his father was "a wealthy soup manufacturer". In fact the family interests extended to a field of comestibles well beyond soup; and indeed during the war in Crimea in 1855, Lancia was the victualler to General Lamarmora; and later did a big trade with a number of central European countries. As to the soup making, it seems likely that someone wishing to make an uncomplimentary reference to his commercial prowess referred to him as a "marchand de Soupe" — which, of course, does not mean soup manufacturer!

However all this is of little importance save for one fact that emerges from it. Lancia senior had for his town house, premises at No 9 Corso Vittorio in Turin. Here he let the ground floor to Giovanni Ceirano, who, together with Faccioli, was building racing cars; and it was here that the young Vincenzo got his taste for the new-fangled motors—to the extent that he more or less walked out of technical school to attach himself to the family's tenant and his business. Lancia himself

Vincenzo Lancia on a race-winning Fiat in 1902

later said "If my father had not had the brilliant idea of renting the place to Gioanin Ceirano I would have remained a nobody". It was also in this workshop that Lancia first met Felice Nazzaro, when they found themselves working side by side with one another.

The Ceirano brothers were among the real founders of the Italian motor industry. There were four of them in all, at least two of them called Giovanni and one further son called Giovanni Ernesto. The one who influences our story, however, is the eldest Giovanni Batista Ceirano; and having joined him in a capacity variously described as bookkeeper and storeman Lancia went with him to Fiat a year later there to be described as chief inspector. None of this makes particular sense; but progress in those days, both for men and ideas, was very rapid indeed and the exact function of the young Lancia is perhaps of only academic interest. Suffice to say that he was at first an office man, and that he quickly transferred himself to the mechanical side of the business, soon becoming

Vincenzo Lancia in the Vanderbilt Cup 1904

CHAPTER ONE

Fiat's chief tester and later joining the great Felice Nazzaro as one of the company's racing drivers. Of that part of his career details come more sensibly in the racing chapters.

In fact it was a very short time before this remarkable young man had set out in business, for in 1906 he left Fiat and started up as a motor manufacturer. Like Bugatti he was something of an eccentric; but unlike Bugatti a trained rather than a "natural" engineer — though he is said to have had 'the ear of a blind man' and to be able to detect the slightest variation in the sound of an engine. He could abide nothing but the best material and the best workmanship; and when displeased with anything he saw would whistle through his teeth a piedmontese "romance" — a sure sign to all and sundry that trouble was coming.

Vincenzo Lancia

Considering he was to be one of the industry's great innovators, his first cars were more than a little conventional; but they were big and powerful and very well made, and did good service among the Allies in the first world war (they were already well known in England). With the arrival of more sophisticated models in the early twenties he used to insist that he wanted a car which would go at walking pace in top gear and then accelerate to over 120 kph. And quite often they would do just that.

Although he started, as did everyone else, making cars for the rich — for only the rich could afford cars anyway — he was also very much a man of his times; and when he made his great break-through with the Lambda it was a car for the middle classes more than anything else. It was certainly not a sports car, for once out on his own, his interest in racing ceased altogether — it was the customers who mattered not the speed. He had a rule that no works driver, out on whatever business, was permitted to overtake another Lancia. Vincenzo held the view that no client must ever get the impression that there was a car faster than his, or a driver more intrepid.

If he moved with the market he also moved with the political dictates of his times. He gave up, when it was expedient to do so, the Greek letters in favour of more obviously Latin names; and his big cars both before and after the war became very much the presidential transport. Lancia, you see, had quality. They may not always have been regarded as one of the *Grandes Marques* and because of it they escaped, perhaps on purpose, some of the high praise lavished on their competitors; but they thereby also escaped a good deal of contumely. Historians of unimpeachable veracity are united in the belief that there were no bad Lancias; and no car to-day carries its pedigree more proudly.

Vincenzo Lancia died in 1937 just as the famous Aprilia came on to the market, but the company survived and after the war with Vittorio Jano, Italy's most distinguished designer on their staff, they produced the first really new model since their founders death, the Aurelia; and later went into Formula One. Up to this time the control of the company was still with the Lancia family, but after the withdrawal of the Grand Prix cars times became difficult and the company passed out of the family's hands. Distinguished cars were still made but the fight was tough. Surprisingly, right at the end of the story, we see how closely knit the Italian industry is, how the few men who founded it have stayed together.

When the moment of need arrived it was Fiat who came to the rescue — the company to whom Vincenzo owed his early fame. In those days as a great "ace" Lancia had known well both Ferrari and Pinin Farina. After Ascari's tragic death it was to Ferrari that the racing cars were sent; and through all the years Farina was near enough the "house" coachbuilder — doing much of his best pre-war work on Lancia chassis. With the new generation of Lancias, under Fiat's sensible and sensitive aegis, the coachwork design is in the hands of Sergio Pininfarina.

It's a small world, one might say, but one in which Lancia has a special place, for the traditions instilled into the company by the special mind of its founder have not been lost.

CHAPTER TWO

Alphabetical beginnings

Things started rather shakily when Vincenzo Lancia decided to become a motor manufacturer. He had taken as a partner a man named Claudio Fogolin whom he had met at Fiat and each had put up half of the meagre 100,000 Lira capital and signed their deeds of agreement on the 29th of November 1906. Having acquired part of the old Itala factory he started production on his first model only to have all the preliminary work destroyed in a fire in February 1907. Replacing the loss used up most of the remaining capital, but Lancia went on undeterred and by mid-September the first chassis was ready to go on the road.

The car was known as the Alpha and was a straight-forward four-cylinder car with a capacity of 2543 cc, side valves and an L-head. It had a four speed gearbox and shaft drive and was good for about 90 kph. Large, stately and not at all sporting, its appeal was quality and dependability — when the latter commodity was in very short supply. This was very soon followed by the Di-Alpha a six-cylinder 3815 cc vehicle of which only 23 were made — some of them of quite a sporting appearance. It was Lancia's only essay at the six-cylinder engine for many years.

After these two cars came a series of fairly closely associated models the Beta, Gamma, and Delta. They had monobloc in line engines, Bosch magnetos and otherwise a conventional layout as before. The Beta had a 3120 cc engine, the Gamma, a year later, one of 3460 cc and finally the Delta was a 4080 cc machine. This same engine went into the Eta of 1913 with electric lighting available as an option, while the following year the 4940 cc Theta featured full electrical equipment as standard, which Lancia claim to be the first car in Europe so fitted.

A number of the large and successful cars, particularly the tourers, saw service as staff cars during the '14-'18 war; and it was during this period that Count Carlo Biscaretti di Ruffia (one of the founders of Fiat and after whom the great motor museum in Turin is now named) designed the emblem of the lance which, superimposed upon a steering wheel, became the firm's badge.

With the peace came the Kappa — a direct development of the Theta. Also in 1919 came a prodigious prototype in the form of a V12 6.1 litre car which appeared at several motor shows, but when costed-out became too expensive to put on the market. However, although this car never came to anything it did provide Lancia with a lot of information about very narrow V engines (this one had only 22° between blocks) which were possible to cast as a monobloc — an idea which was to be a powerful influence on his later designs.

Then we have the last pair of conventional cars in the ohv 4940 cc Dikappa and lastly the ohc 4594 cc Trikappa. These were big expensive cars for big expensive people, who in a time of general financial depression were in somewhat short supply. Vincenzo Lancia therefore turned his mind to other things — a car that would uphold his engineering standards but have a wider appeal than the rather eclectic, though wholly excellent, models he was then engaged in making — and by 1922 he was ready to take the dust sheets off one of the most exciting cars in the history of motoring — whether one's standpoint be practical or mechanical.

The original Alpha was in production for a number of years. The car in front of the castle on the left is sometimes called the first Lancia, but in fact that was a tourer. The engine dated 1908 is likewise from a later example.

The Alpha and Dialpha both appeared in competition guise — as what might be called the European equivalent to the "raceabout".

Above, the 1909 Beta in open Italian style and below it, the rather more staid British version by Maythorn (also 1909). Bottom, the Gamma was a very logical development. All the early Lancias follow a clear Lancia line.

Another Gamma, of 1911.

A post-war (1919) picture of a pre-war car. A Maythorn coupé on the Delta chassis.

The Epsilon was a development of the Delta with the same engine measurements. The differences are minimal. Below, the Eta has a longer stroke and a five litre capacity, more suited to heavy coachwork.

The Theta above and the Kappa below, suddenly look much more up to date probably because of the higher radiator and bonnet line.

Two Kappas, above a very English looking but in fact Italian tourer and below another Maythorn body, this time an open drive limousine.

More Kappas, a very eccentric sports tourer from the Autocar of 1919 and, below, two tourers the bottom one having the addition of occasional seats.

The more usual tourer with centre bar behind front seats and the usual optional extra of a folding screen for the protection of the rear passengers.

An early Trikappa photographed recently outside the Biscaretti Museum and below two contemporary views with the all weather equipment on show.

A similar car to the one on the opposite page but in light colour and below, an H. J. Mulliner landaulette with very fine pillars giving an exceptional view for the time.

Above, the almost mythical 12-cylinder from the 1919 Paris and London Shows and below, probably another experimental car of which nothing is known.

CHAPTER THREE

The Lambda Breakthrough

No one can look at the history of motoring without seeing the Lancia Lambda as a major technical milestone. Leaving aside its novel engine, its independent suspension, and a whole host of other minor innovations, its unique unitary construction, in which body and chassis were one, came a good ten years before Mr. Budd succeeded in selling his idea for a monocoque to Andre Citroen.

Exactly how and why Lancia came to make the Lambda the way he did, is not really clear. There is a splendid romantic story about his having thought of it when travelling in a boat — which must be given about as much credence as the one concerning George Stephenson and the boiling kettle. On the other hand the advance in metallurgical knowledge brought about by the First World War had many people experimenting with welded up presswork; and Lancia's own concern with, for example, armoured cars could only have led his mind in a similar direction. An engineer to his fingertips he would have been very much abreast of current thought; and being his own master was in a position to innovate, when the spirit moved him.

Without in any way denigrating his genius, the idea, as he put it into practice, was a simple one. A light chassis was given strength by extending the sides upwards to form a basic body — pierced only to provide the smallest of doors which were then an acceptable, if inconvenient, fashion. (Shades of the famous Frazer-Nash remark "doors, doors, what on earth d'yer want doors for?). When it came to providing closed coachwork Lancia came to a sensible expedient that the rest of the motoring world only discovered a whole World War later — the "hard top".

This light construction was powered by a four-cylinder narrow V engine of just over 2 litres capacity, which gave it a satisfactory, if not startling, performance. This coupled with independent front suspension, on a sliding pillar system not unlike that used in Great Britain by Morgan, together with a comfortably long wheelbase made not only for good handling but plenty of space as well. In a nutshell, an excellent touring car, which was exactly what Lancia was aiming at.

Of course things did not stand still; and many changes were incorporated before the last of the ninth series Lambdas left the works in 1931, after about 13,000 examples had been made. The principal changes were as follows. The cubic capacity was put up to 2.4 litres for the seventh series, introduced in 1926; and further increased to 2.6 litres with the eight series in 1928. The cars started with three speed gearboxes, but a four speed model was introduced in 1925 for the fifth series.

The limitations of the system only became apparent as time went on, for with the revival of fortunes in Italy there was a considerable demand for custom built bodies; and Lancia's good friend and coachbuilder, Pinin Farina, was hamstrung by the monocoque. For this reason a separate chassis version was offered with the seventh series and the eighth and ninth series in fact had a separate chassis anyway —

which is perhaps why enthusaists lay so much store by the "seventh Series Lambda" since this was the last, and most highly developed version, of the original fascinating concept.

The success of the later series Lambdas, especially when fitted with custom coachwork, led Lancia back to the idea of building a high class luxury car — and the success of the Lambda name no doubt led him to christen his new model the Dilambda. This was a V8 (in the same narrow V) but with a separate and conventional chassis. Independent suspension, servo brakes (on the later models) together with such little luxuries as centralised chassis lubrication and twin electric fuel pumps, brought it very much into line with the thinking behind many of the more successful sports saloons of the mid-thirities, such as the Derby Bentleys which it preceded by some years.

Here we see the Lancia as a class car, with, as like as not elegant coachwork by an outside firm, and a limited but demanding public. In all about 1700 Dilambdas were made; but they led to a succession of fine cars, notably the Astura before the war and the Flaminia after it. One part of the Lancia image was confirmed. But lest anyone should think that innovation was over, or that the small car had lost its place in his mind, Lancia was already at work on a car which the public might see as a successor to the Lambda, rather than a development of it.

LAMBDA

The original Lambda prototype photographed by Lancia himself on the Mont Cenis – 1st September 1921.

The Bugatti style radiator and the Prototype Lambda with and without its "hard top". The design of the chassis made this the only practical way of providing a closed car — until it was decided to produce an ordinary flat chassis for coachbuilders.

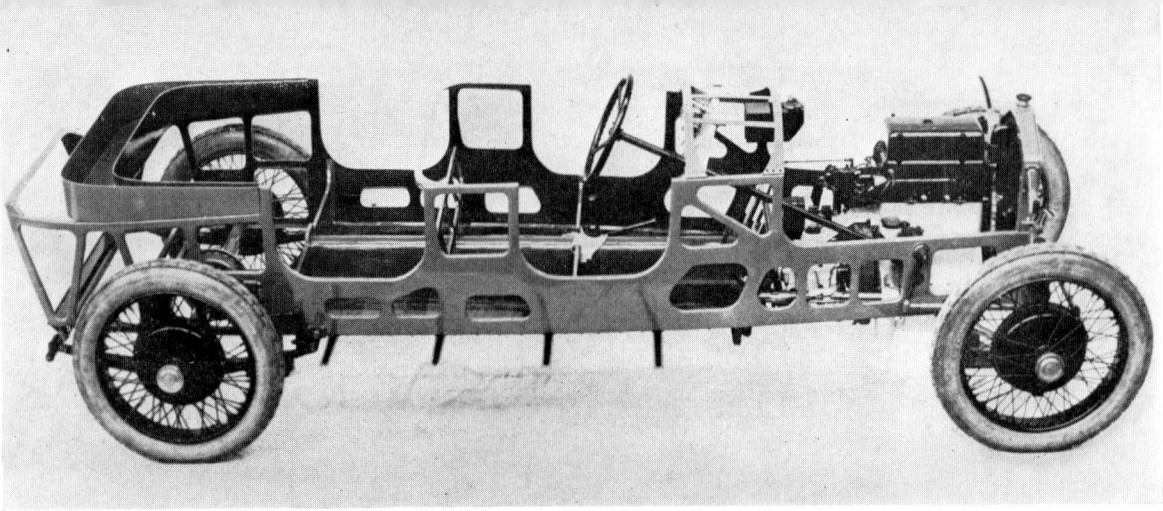

The Lambda chassis in all its glory and an early 1st Series Lambda (1922/23) on the wooden "tyres" they used in the factory.

Virtually the same car with its
hard top fixed. The series numbers
were for photographic identification
at a later date — but no one now
seems to know exactly what they
identify.

98 10 02

The same thing with proper tyres and without curtains in the saloon. Not the same car, of course, but both 1st Series.

A 2nd Series car — this time with half a hard top providing the then fashionable "let the chauffeur get wet" configuration.

4th Series showing minor modifications to the wings and doors now hinged at the front – though no bigger.
Also said to be 4th Series — this car with its fat tyres is a currently existent example which appears to have been modified over the years.

5th Series — the open model with the forerunner of the 'dog-leg' windscreen.

Here come the coachbuilders, a neat Spider (just chop away at the back) by Casaro dated 1925. (5th Series).

The 6th Series, now with much bigger doors.

A Lambda instrument panel (6th Series) and the hardtop now a more permanent saloon. The old "Ballon Smontabile" has become "Semirigido della casa".

A Lambda Sport by Casaro made in late 1926.

Examples of the standard 7th Series saloon and tourer.

For the first time a chassis was made available to coachbuilders, but this Spider has so many signs of Lancia's own style that one must assume it is of works manufacture. Note the small square door for the golf-bags, introduced from America.

A 1928 example of the Lambda Sport by Casaro.

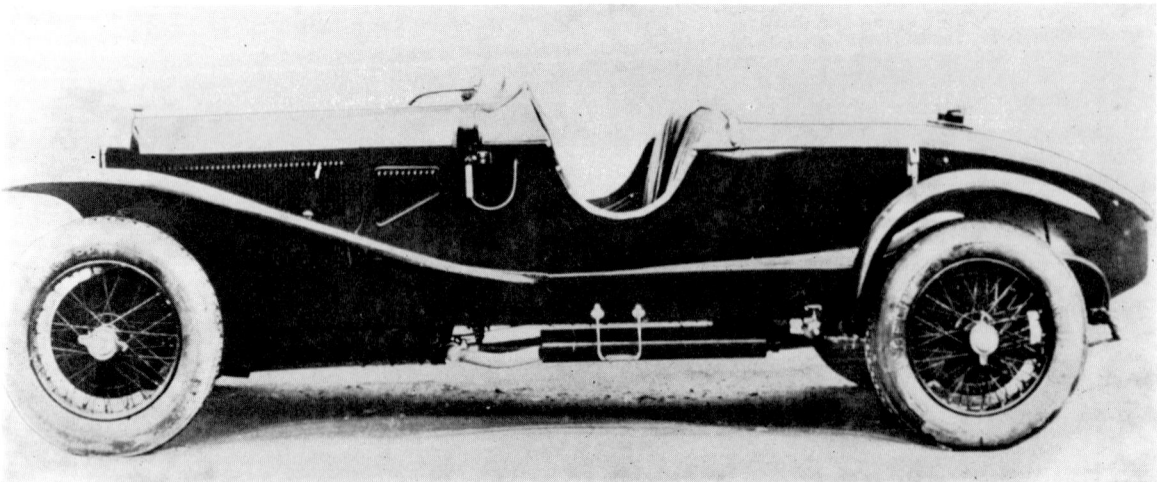

The Airway *saloon by* Albany Coachworks *1928. There was an earlier and even more curious three-seater version, and a rather formal (by comparison) Weymann saloon.*

LANCIA
1928

From the 8th Series onwards the Lambda had a chassis and here it is — no less robust than the original monocoque concept, it is more practical and less inhibiting to the progress of body design. Above is the 8th Series engine.

Three coupés. Top and bottom are not identical but both are of course Weymann — the hood irons do not in this instance betoken a drop head, but the centre car does open and although fabric bodied is more like James Young than anyone else.

Three more Lambdas. The saloon in the centre is a 1929 Weymann as is the tourer below although the coachbuilder has been at great pains to copy the authentic Lancia shape as seen in the top picture.

DILAMBDA

The Dilambda chassis — a very robust affair, the side members in the engine compartment echoing Lambda practice.

The Dilambda was a logical extension up-market of the very successful Lambda. Here it is in 1932 with a now forgotten celebrity.
Below, a slightly earlier Torpedo.

Stabilimenti Farina (the "old" firm) with German overtones and a touch of the British Doctor's coupé.

A 1931 Pinin Farina design.
Below, a rare Castagna — the belt of colour across the scuttle was very indicative of the house style. The high radiator prevents the car from having the exquisite line of similar bodies on, say, the Alfa Romeo chassis.

An unknown saloon dated 1930 probably H. J. Mulliner as the low built line and trunk fixings compare with that at the bottom of the page.

A Weymann landaulette de ville and an H. J. Mulliner saloon.

Again certainly built under Weymann patents (plate between the doors) and possibly H. J. Mulliner but ample evidence anyway of Lancia's hold on the top end of the British market.

Top and bottom, two more Weymanns of 1930 — this time by Weymann Motor Bodies (1925) Ltd. — and looking very like the Stutz of the period — or should we say the Stutz looked very like a Lancia.

Murphy looking duller than usual on its all too familiar background.

The Arnaulet sports saloon by Wm. Arnold of Manchester made its Olympia debut in 1930; but this car may well be some years later.

Above, a real doctor's coupé (probably H. J. Mulliner) and below a Weymann of almost identical design to the Stutz.

A short chassis Dilambda saloon with fashionable removable trunks.

Coachbuilder unknown but a "1932 Show Model 2-door saloon", and below a neat and compact John Charles body of the same period.

A rather splendid Pinin Farina saloon made in series in the fashionable "pillarless" style.

Two more examples — the lower having the addition of a trunk fitted into the space provided by the removal of the boot-lid.

A more elegant two-door version, a year later than the saloon — 1933.
Below, a cabriolet looking very large indeed, but perhaps the lady occupants were particularly petite.

Looking for all the world like the extinct Autovia, it is a British body of 1934 — very likely by Arthur Mulliner.

Above, an Abbey saloon by C. R. Abbott Ltd., and below another John Charles design which appears in several guises and on a number of different chassis.

A rare format. A tidy coupé de ville by Farina.

More high-jinks with the boot-trunk. Pinin Farina, of course, who never let a good idea go unused.

Below, dated 1936 and attributed to Pinin Farina, this Dilambda looks like a very late effort as the Astura was well in production by the time.

CHAPTER FOUR

Vincenzo Lancia - the final analysis

With the Dilambda established as a leader among the world's fine cars, Lancia once more turned away from the grand towards the practical; and in 1933, a little more than ten years after he had launched the Lambda, he came up with his first small "family" car the Augusta. Society was on the move and Everyman in Italy, as much as anywhere else in the world, was on the verge of becoming a motorist. Once again Lancia went back to unitary construction — this time a little boxy saloon of 'pillarless' design, that is to say with the doors closing together in the centre of the car and without a central pillar, which made entry into the rear seats a great deal easier. It was very far from fast, Lancia's themselves claiming only a modest 102 kph, which we can accept as usually just under 60 mph on an ordinary road. It handled well however and was well liked; but what is much more important, it paved the way for the subsequent Aprilia.

Lancias limited numbers allowed them to keep older models in production while others were developed; and it also allowed for the gradual development — one might almost say expansion — of any particular model in the existing range. It is therefore rather difficult to put the production into sensible chronological perspective, because of the overlap of models.

In 1931 the company had offered two new cars — one of which was to become one of the great Lancias of all time, and the other very much a stop-gap. Whether they were planned this way, or whether fate, in the guise of the market place, finally decreed it, we shall never know.

The Astura which was to grow into one of the most important cars, started life rather modestly as a replacement for the Dilambda, which was still in production when it was announced in 1931. At that time it had the usual narrow V8 engine of only 2604 cc, which produced a modest 73 bhp giving the car a maximum speed of about 125 kph. Its smaller brother, the Artena, announced in the same year, was a four-cylinder model of just under 2 litres. These two cars mark the break from the Greek Alphabet which some sources say was running out; but as they had only got as far as Lambda this seems to lack likelyhood, even in the face of a commercial vehicle called the Ro (Rho, if you want to be Oxford Dictionary about it). But times were on the move — intense Italian Nationalism was in the air; and a new generation of motorists was in the showrooms to whom Greek was just Greek.

While the Artena quickly passed from our ken, the Astura went from strength to strength, growing to 3 litres, and gaining servo operation for the brakes. In later years it was fitted with some of the most handsome coachwork of the pre-war period, and was widely adopted as the official government transport for high dignitaries of the Mussolini regime.

While this was happening at the top of the range, a chassis was made for the little Augusta so that special bodies could also be fitted to that; but its lack of performance was an inhibiting factor on sales. It made many friends in Great Britain however, and a number of British Coachbuilders produced bodies for it —

its rather square shape commending itself to the national tastes of this damp island.

But while the British were squaring with the Augusta, and Pinin Farina and his colleagues were rounding-off the Astura, Vincenzo Lancia was back in the innovative realms of his fertile mind. He wanted to see the end of the three-box car, he wanted to combine lightness with space, economy with speed, handling with common sense — to make a car which would be all things to all men, to fulfil in fact, an engineers dream. At this point he seems to be very much the precursor of Alec Issigonis — and when his chick was hatched it was indeed an engineer's ugly duckling. It was called Aprilia.

Shortly after it first appeared in 1937 Vincenzo Lancia died. As a man he had contributed much to motoring, he had set standards by which many other cars were and would always be judged. Simplicity he would accept, shoddyness he abhorred. Goodness knows what kind of memorial he would have liked — Giovanni Agnelli when unveiling a bust of him in the works said "This factory of his, which is famous throughout the world, does honour to Italian industry"; but that we can to-day still write "Lancia never made a bad car" is perhaps the greatest tribute of all.

The little Aprilia started life with a developed Augusta engine of 1325 cc, which in its new, light, truly monocoque shell, weighing only 1804 lbs, gave the car a speed of nearly 80 mph. Synchromesh you did not get; but the rewards for learning to use the excellent little gearbox well, were ample. It had independent suspension all round and a streamline shape that gave it around 30 mpg. Later the engine was bored out to 1486 cc and various other improvements made, so that the car looked more solid and had a much less frugal dashboard. Of course it was no time before a "punt" had to be produced for friend Farina and his ilk, and although they much improved on the designers original appearance, it was the Standard Aprilia saloon that had the charm from the drivers point of view.

It stayed in production until after the second World War; and just before that disaster burst upon them, the company produced the Aprilia's little brother in the form of the 'Ardea' — a 903 cc small version of the Aprilia, with a five speed gearbox and as much impudence as the Astura had dignity.

ASTURA

The Astura, as it first appeared in 1931. About as unlike the startling Farina creations of seven years later as it is possible to imagine.

A 1933/34 chassis. The sloping radiator belongs to the second series officially introduced in 1934, but many of the cars carry 1933 dates.
Below, the standard six light saloon of the first series — an almost totally American concept.

A two-door coupé which we have seen before on the Dilambda — save that the doors now open at the front.

Although photographed outside the Abbey Coachworks factory at Park Royal, London in 1934 it does not necessarily mean the body is by Abbey, but it is obviously British built.
Below, the 1934 standard saloon — a little less like an Austin Sixteen than the original but still nothing to write home about in terms of beauty.

A Viotti of Turin sports tourer body shown at the 1932 Olympia Motor Show — gaudy but fun.

A John Charles streamlined saloon very similar to their body on the Dilambda but with more headroom at the back, and a less lovely line because of it.

A rather unlikely looking Doctor's coupé — this time by Pinin Farina and therefore incorporating his almost obsessional waist moulding.

The March bodied Astura of 1935, much heavier and less delightful looking than the Augusta version.

A standard Italian saloon — offered in England by Kevill-Davies & March.

And in 1937 from the same agent an obviously non-standard model — coachbuilder unknown though the distinctive rear quarter should give a clue.

A 1936 Pinin Farina fixed head coupé which should be compared with the last of the Dilambdas — it is the same year.

An unusual Pinin Farina two-door four light drophead. A really horrid confusion of styles, but a very well-padded hood of almost German splendour.

Five photographs of similar cars.
All of them Pinin Farina and all
resemble the car recently owned by
Michael Scott, and featured in the
frontispiece, also seen here in the
centre photograph.

Two Farina drop-heads. The car above was built for Count "Johnny" Lurani and that below exhibited at the Paris Salon of 1935.

Two more Farinas. Above, the rear standard four-door cabriolet (see the saloon on the following page) and below, a more individual two-door design.

One of the Astura limousines much used by High Government officials of the time. They looked better with discs on the wheels. Pinin Farina, of course.

And the combination of the boot/trunk theme brought up to date by Pinin Farina in what was nearly a "standard" saloon.

A somewhat offbeat coupé de ville (Pinin Farina) which must have looked very dashing when the de ville extension was folded away.

A year later, 1939, the same coachbuilder lacks the courage of his convictions; but produces a more acceptable design.

Four Farina foursome coupés, one fixed head and three convertibles, all displaying the same design characteristics and intermingling ideas.

The fixed head is by far the most tasteful, but the light coloured drop-head perhaps the most interesting as it was made for the 1938 Berlin Show.

Farina played endless variations on all his themes, all interesting, but tending to bear out the nursery rhyme on the opposite page.

There was a little girl, who had a little curl, right in the middle of her forehead, when she was good, she was very very good; but when she was bad she was horrid.

A very "Brighton front" effort by Pinin Farina (1939). It looked a good deal more exciting and less vulgar in its day than it does now. Below, is also Pinin Farina in the same year and almost certainly the car parked behind in the previous picture.

ARTENA

The introduction of the Artena in
1931 was a move in the direction of
the popular car — and it looked just
that. The chassis was commendably
solid and the no nonsense 2 litre
engine put common sense and quality
before performance.

This one is accredited to Stabilimenti Farina, a four-door pillarless saloon.

Pinin Farina in his British Vein — a simple "sportsmans coupé" lightened by bright beading round the wings.

Two rather similar versions of the Pinin Farina cabriolet which add a little elegance.

Its that line again — although in the bottom picture Farina has given it up to produce another on very British lines.

An elegant little sedanca coupé by James Young shown at the 1932 London Motor Show. Below, another British built body, a drop-head coupé with a 3 position hood, two years later than the above car.

AUGUSTA

The standard Augusta saloon — almost unrecognisable in this unusual paint job — black wings and plain sombre colours were the order of the day.

Farina, a "faux cabriolet" — or fixed-head close coupled coupé to the pedantic British.

And a real cabriolet; but no makers plate and no caption makes identification uncertain.

Looking long for an Augusta — this Abbey example from late '34 is very Alvis looking.

The "March Special" sports tourer offered at £450 at the 1934 Motor Show. Kevill-Davies & March sold quite a few at what was then a not inconsiderable price.

Sadly one only had to put the hood up to spoil the whole effect.

John Charles was responsible for
the top car probably called
"futuristic" in its time,
Whittingham and Mitchell under-
took the construction of the centre
car for Norman Edwards and
John Charles only followed the
prevailing fashion for the last of
the trio.

APRILIA

The original Aprilia — not a thing of beauty but all the same a joy for ever. Vincenzo Lancia's last car.

With "improvements" by Farina, which show that you can gild a lily but not an ugly duckling — the manufacturer's improvements in the second version (below) did much more for it.

*Above the "Bilux" — a design study and below a series saloon — both Farina of course.
The roof trunk enjoyed a brief vogue.*

More Farina — still accepting the pressures of countless design ideas — Renault, for example, in the one below.

The second version of the Pinin Farina "Bilux".

Boneschi makes very good Travelling Shops and Public Transport bodies, but no one could call this Aprilia inspired.

Below, a 1948 Pinin Farina saloon. Bigger and better but not so striking. By this time Pinin Farina was settling down into the easy production of immaculate shapes on which his post-war reputation was built.

Kevill-Davies & March again. From the '37 show the sports 2/4 seater open tourer. Price £465 (it had a dickey).

The 1939 Pinin Farina Spider and below with competition in mind the Pinin Farina "Aprilia Aerodinamica".

The colossal variation in scope in the Farina design of the time leave one breathless. The model below had serious competition intentions and the two above are both called aerodinamica also.

This is March again — and the central window holders did fold.

For a change Ghia — and a few came to England in 1938 where they were very much admired as the new Italian line.

A 1939 four-seater cabriolet of rather conventional design.

A similar car to the above with a more fashionable front. Some like this arrived in London before the war and were also much sought after. Which came first we wonder.
Below, with an extended steering column and the two seats near the back axle the impression of length and speed is startling. Farina at his best.

Two very similar Pinin Farina drop-head coupés, undated but one would guess post-war, for their likeness to certain Pinin Farina designs on Alfa Romeo at that time.

Again after the war when Farina had had enough of frills and was developing as in the 1949 car below a definitive style with great strength of line.

Drawings from the 2nd Series Aprilia catalogue.

ARDEA

The Ardea was so clearly Aprilia's little brother that there is little more to be said beyond deploring the "motif" on the front. Below, like London, Rome has its own ideas about Taxis — and here is Lancia's version of it.

CHAPTER FIVE

Picking up the pieces

The post war years in Europe were not a very happy time for anyone — least of all the Italians; and the process of getting the country back into any kind of economic shape was a long and tedious one. Money was short and materials shorter, and while high spirits could be bought by the bottle, sober judgement made manufacturers cautious beings. Like everyone else Lancia went back into production with the cars they had had before the war, and which were the last legacies of their founder. By 1950 there was both the desire and the need for a new model and Gianni Lancia, one of the founders two sons, who was then running the company, had acquired the services of no less a person than Vittorio Jano — the designer among other things of the P3 Alfa Romeo.

In retrospect one is inclined to wonder where the force of influence lay. Did Gianni Lancia get hold of Jano because he had the bug of competition stirring within him — or did he acquire Jano simply because he wanted the best available designer, only to discover that designers of Jano's quality have the need for competition buried in their souls. It is unlikely that we shall ever know. At all events Jano's first efforts for Lancia were not exactly redolent of the Grand Prix scene.

The new car, known as the Aurelia continued much of the Lancia tradition in terms of its independent front suspension (by then the system, not the fact, was unusual) and it also used in its standard form a Lancia type "hull". The engine was a narrow V6 of 1754 cc with push rods for the ohv rather than the pre-war camshafts. The gearbox was part of the back axle and the shape commendably Lancia though there were signs that the master's abhorrence of the three box car were being overlooked. Only a year later the car was made available with the more powerful two litre engine and the first short chassis "GT" Coupé styled by Farina appeared. This was soon joined by a "spyder" and with these cars, and no Vincenzo Lancia to hold a contrary opinion, the company went into motoring competition as the dictates of marketing at that time seemed to demand it. Just how well they did is part of another chapter; but in terms of the general story another chapter was also opening up.

Once this car was launched the firm turned, indeed as Lancia himself had always done, to the more utilitarian type of vehicle; and in 1953 the little Ardea was replaced by an 1100 cc model called the Appia. Externally it still followed the family shape — Lancias rounded back having a slight "notch" though the family resemblance remained strong. In the fulness of time this car too was developed so that it could carry specialist coachwork; but its engine was not allowed to get any bigger.

Despite the success in the world of sport the Lancia fortunes were sinking, and indeed it seems somewhat incredible, in retrospect, that they should have launched themselves into Formula One at all. Of course, we all know that Grand Prix racing is a powerful drug, its rewards can be great; but they are more usually the rewards of reputation that those of rising share values. As it was, the Appia which itself cost a good deal to develop, was not a great profit maker (small cars seldom are) and it was profits they needed rather than reputation which they already had. The sports car racing was one thing; but then came the sad business of the entry into Formula One with the Jano designed cars. Ascari's death was a great blow; and the cars were handed over to Ferrari, while amid the gloom the Lancia family lost control of the company. So often when this kind of thing has happened, all that the firm stood for is lost; but badge engineering was somehow avoided and new life put into the dying organisation. One of the principal contributors to this injection of vitality was an Aurelia based car — a handsome four-seater four-door Coupé — which Farina had called the Florida (the Italian coachbuilding industry was obsessed with America at the time); and it was a factory built version of this car known as the Flaminia which was to turn the tide.

AURELIA

The 1950 B.10 Aurelia in its
original Saloon form following very
much the current Lancia shape as
well as the engineering principles.
Centre, the V6 engine — long before
Ford or Volvo got hold of the idea;
and below, one of the few Woodies
to come out of Italy, the Giardinetta.

A fairly hideous long-chassis version, but not really half-as-bad as it looks, due to careless photography, where the reflections spoil the side moulding.

Below, a 5/6 seater saloon by Pinin Farina using many of the larger coupés design details — not quite happy but better looking and more roomy than the standard car.

Variations on a theme. The top car is the second version with neater lines while below is a dark car with chromium mouldings to the order of a Mr. Wrightsman and beneath it looking less gaudy with minor changes to the grill is the last of the line.

A 1952 fixed-head coupé by the ever present Pinin Farina. Below, a year later and the design has been modified to produce a most handsome motor car.

Cabriolet Aurelia 2000
Scala 1:10

A Michelotti design for Vignale and below the fixed-head version in the flesh. No pictures of the drop-head can be found but the rear wing treatment alone demands its inclusion.

Another Vignale effort this time by Ford Anglia out of Standard Vanguard as far as the eye can tell. And below a more conventional effort from the same shop.

Starting at the Turin Show in 1952 Pinin Farina was carried away by the shape of jet engine intakes. As like as not the origins were American (Ghia were up to the same thing) but here is the first of a long series. The Spyder 200 on the Aurelia B52 — note the top outline of the windscreen. A year later, 1953, it was even more stark, but the wind deflecting screen remained a feature.

Three versions of the coupé PF 200, top, as a 2 + 2, with excellent all-round vision, centre, the 1954 version with better lines but probably poor visibility. Having dropped the strange device before the rear wheels on the lower cars (which are earlier) Farina then puts it back. Bell ringers have nothing on Farina when it comes to ringing changes.

Top, a more elegant open version
Centre, the 1954 coupé PF 200—
no it is not the same as any of the
preceeding cars and bottom, a close
relative of the top car if not an
identical model. Anywas the 1953
cabriolet PF 200.

The B24 Spider, one of Farina's immortal Lancias — well on the way to being a collector's piece. And below a similar convertible with a more "civilized" windscreen and wind-up windows.

Three versions of the Aurelia coupé which followed the Spider. All are similar but have detail differences. Above, the 2nd Series; below, the 4th Series (1954/5) and on the opposite page the 1957 version.

Below, "Lancia Aurelia Berlina, Florida" magic words. One of Pinin Farina's really outstanding designs — which led, of course, to the production Flaminia.

Three Vignale designs which at least make a change from the perpetual Pinin. The top is a refinement of the car a few pages back. Vignale had their own ideas about Lancia Radiators. On the middle a rather messey drop head (show reflections don't help) and below, acquiescence to contemporary feeling for air intakes.

APPIA

The little Appia introduced in
1953 was, with its 1089 cc engine,
clearly a replacement for the
Ardea, but like all other small
Lancias it grew up very quickly.
Here it is in its original form.

Zagato, like Farina, sometimes "worked over" a standard model — usually, as here to good effect. This lower car poses problems — its rear end is Series II but the front looks like Series I — Series I$\frac{1}{2}$ perhaps?

A Pinin Farina Coupé on the 2nd
Series developement introduced in
1957. Once again American
influence is strong and there are
shades of Nash Metropolitan.
The 3rd Series (1959) — dull looking
but in the Italian tradition of its
time. While Vignale came up with a
rather handsome four-seater two
door saloon.

Vignale also introduced the convertible — complete with hardtop and whitewalls, and hardly distinguishable from a Fiat.

While Pinin Farina replied with a scaled down version of the Flaminia.

Zagato in one of their less eccentric moods came up with these two. The top one is something of a mystery, the lower is just called G.T.E.

Appia Sport Zagato is all Lancia have to say about this bunch; but they could well be the same as the top car on the facing page.

CHAPTER SIX

The Flaminia and a new generation

Throughout all the years of Lancia production the bond between the company and the house of Pininfarina (as we must now learn to call it) was as close as the original bond between Vincenzo Lancia and his friend Batista "Pinin" Farina; and nowhere was it more marked than in the last days of the Astura before the war, when some truly magnificent models were on offer. In fact, however, these were chassis clothed by an eminent coachbuilder (and there were others of eminence besides Farina) and not factory products — there were still perfectly ordinary, and visually rather dull, Asturas to be had in return for a cheque.

This process was resumed after the war with the Aurelia; and it was at the Turin Show in the autumn of 1955 that Farina showed his "Florida" based on an Aurelia chassis. It was by the standards of its day a supremely lovely car — and now bids fair to be a classic. Such was its success that the company, whose affairs were at a low ebb, decided to take a chance and make a factory version of the same thing. This they did and the Flaminia was born.

The Flaminia used the same 2.5 litre engine and the rear-axle-cum-gearbox that was then established as Lancia tradition. It broke new ground with its body shell which had, for Lancia, a new form of unitary construction; and the independent front suspension was no longer by the time honoured sliding pillar system but by a new coil-and-wishbone design of more modern conception. The car was an immediate success and by 1958 the company had introduced a short chassis GT model. Disc brakes were standard and in 1963 the capacity was increased to 2775 cc.

Very soon a true Coupé appeared, and later a GT Coupé in smaller and lighter form — and finally the Flaminia Sport. Meanwhile, back at the works, innovation was once again the order of the day for Dr. Fessia, who had made a name for himself at Fiat before the war (he had been largely responsible for the "Topolino" among other things), had joined the company and was working on the design of their newest effort, the Flavia. This was a little less original that it might have seemed, for all its front-wheel-drive and OHV flat-four engine. Students of automobile history were quick to recognise traces of an earlier 'experimental' car produced by the Caproni aeroplane company just after the war, which had also been designed by the ubiquitous Fessia. All the same it was new ground to Lancia, and helped to develop their then expanding market.

In 1964 the little Appia was dropped (by the time they had finished with it, it was not so little; but that's another story) and in its place came the Fulvia. Originally a rather square looking saloon, again FWD, but with the "old" V-4 engine, it was rapidly developed into a series of attractive coupés; and soon led the Lancia Rally Teams back to the top of the tree. As if to show that nepotism can only be allowed to go so far, and that even Lancia realised there were other coachbuilders beside Farina, they joined with Zagato in a series of the most odd-looking cars that have ever been offered to the public. No one can really say they were ugly (it's a matter of opinion anyway) but they were odd. Functional perhaps, light certainly, and definitely different. They did not add much to the Fulvia's reputation, but they did widen the scope.

We find Lancia now a long way from the Greek alphabet, with three cars called Flaminia, Flavia, and Fulvia, and sales going up. In 1964 they sold 30,000 cars which is good going for a firm that could, with justification, call itself a specialist manufacturer; and it was a great advance on the 8,794 cars they turned out in 1958. All the same the way ahead was a stony one and in fact they were badly in need of some kind of rescue operation. At this point Fiat stepped into the breach (with some help from the government) and before long a new range of cars was on the way.

As with many of these mergers in to-day's world of business it was not a straight-forward take-over; but a more government inspired union. There were tales that Giovanni Agnelli wanted a good name for his up-market operation, to put against BMW and Alfa-Romeo; but this must be fair-to-middling nonsense for the Fiat name was quite good enough. In any event Fiat were the principal creditors, so that in the event Fiat paid just over 1 lire for each of Lancias 1000 Lira shares. Described in some circles as a "Machiavellian discourse" it included most of Italy's financial houses, the government and the Pope — since the Vatican owned one third of the shares. Beyond that a kind of moratorium was declared, Agnelli announcing that he didn't know when they would be paying out the creditors; but promising that it would not be very soon.

One thing only was certain and that was that in future the world markets would be aggressively attacked; and as a first earnest of their intent Lancias went back into the U.S. market with the first of the new cars — the Beta.

FLAMINIA

Having thought up the Florida and designed the Flaminia (top) for Lancia to build, Pinin Farina was quickly back on the scene with the Flaminia coupé (centre).

A Sports version soon followed and here is the 1962 Flaminia G.T. 2500 convertible by — wait for it — Superleggera Touring.

Then Zagato had a go with what must be regarded as their most restrained design ever. The interior, particularly, being typical of Italian thought at the time.

Unidentified save for Motto Torino on the scuttle this is clearly Virgil Exner inspired, though not Vauxhall engined. Not perhaps Lancia's happiest moment.

In contrast to this curiosity however, Touring designed a coupé on the same lines as their drop-head, to put shape on the performance — a desirable and exceptional car.

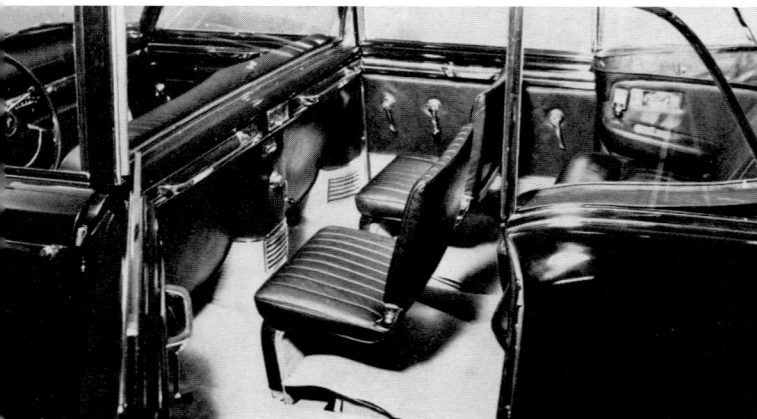

State cars are usually interesting because of their rarity if nothing else, and this Flaminia Presidenziale is no exception. Farina and Lancia could between them be expected to produce a suitable car and this they did. Better looking than almost anything of its kind since Hitler's "Mercs" they are an object lesson in automobile dignity.

FLAVIA

The Flavia announced in 1963
was a middle of the road model
and followed the firm's established
outline for the rather dull family
saloons but it looked and was a
remarkably solid motor.

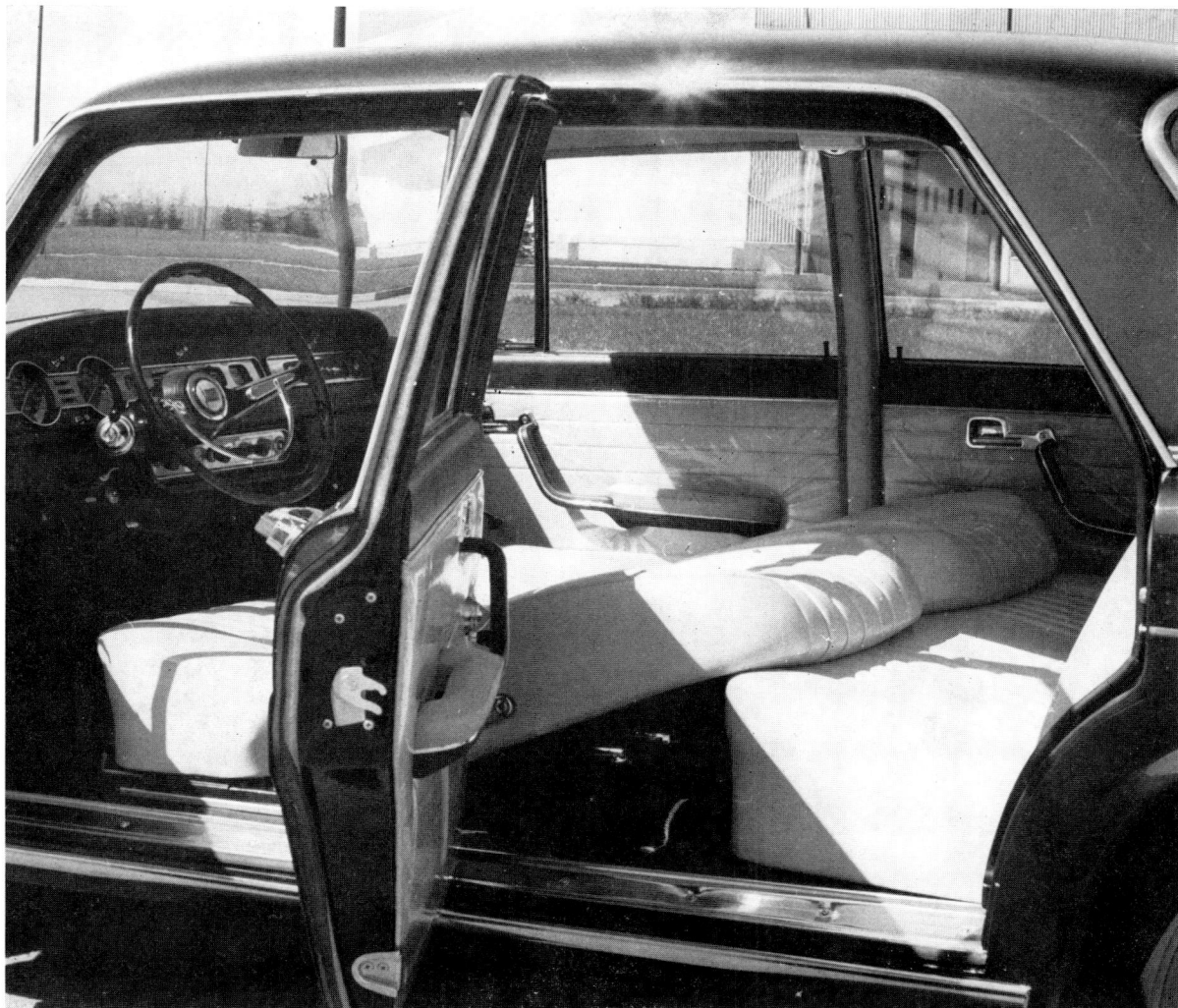

The interior, although severe in the Italian manner was quite luxurious, even the rubber floor seeming sensible rather than frugal. Those Ford Zephyr arm rests plus grab handles were becoming quite a fashion.

Pinin Farina chipped in with a coupé in his usual style.

And Zagato with one of his unusual confections. And later a very handsome "dream car".

Vignale produced the drop-head — a neat car echoing Lancia's taste for severity.

FULVIA

The "little" Fulvia was announced in 1964. And was really aimed at broadening the firm's market — frankly a mass produced family car, it was to lead on to the company's great competition successes.
Comfortable austerity was the keynote to the interior with reclining seats and full equipment but no nonsense.

This was followed by the GTE
with a little more of everything
except good looks. Though the
interior was improved — below,
the 2nd Series car.

And here is the famous coupé of which there were so many almost the same but really quite different versions. This is the first, the 1.2 standard model.

Now comes the 1966 H.F.

The car as it appeared at the 1967 Geneva show — with interior shots which would go for many of the variations.

*Three shots of the Rallye 1.3S —
you really need the back view with all
the writing on it before you know
what your're looking at. Some cars
had flared wings, and bonnet straps
as extras.*

One to catch all but the most well informed. The Fulvia Safari — and if you can contend with the curious typography, it is written on the car.

Engine units of the 1.3S 2nd Series and the 1.6 H.F.

The 1600 H.F. surprisingly came in September 1970 with the 2nd Series generally.

While all this was going on Zagato was having its own ideas. Firstly the Fulvia Sport 1.3S — a very rational design for the coachbuilder.

Whatever one may think of the shape it certainly provides dramatic photographs.

Then came the 2nd Series 1.3S by the same coachbuilder.

And lastly the 1600 Sport.

Then the classiest of them all the Fulvia 3 coupé.

2000

The Lancia 2000 was very much a back to the box effort. Well made and neatly finished few hearts would have missed a beat when this flashed past, but as usual Farina cheered it up with his customary coupé — and the inside was very smart.

CHAPTER SEVEN

Back to the beginning

In an age when people are apparently content with expressions such as "Multi-National Conglomerates", it is not to be expected that a maker of Gentlemen's Motor Cars would have much more luck than a maker of Gentlemen's English; and so not unexpectedly we find Lancia in trouble. Pitted against American money and Japanese effort they faced a seemingly impossible situation in the world's market place.

However, the age of miracles is not passed, and as we have seen Mirafiore was the fount of this one. Egged on by government sources Fiat were persuaded to take the ailing Lancia under their wing. It was a long standing association, and there was much to commend it; but on the face of it one wondered just what sort of new Lancia would emerge. The miracle was that it was the old Lancia that emerged — new in every detail perhaps, and using an engine that had Fiat parentage stamped all over it; but the car was unmistakably a Lancia. One can only assume that it was the Trade Descriptions Act which forbade the use of the first letter of the Greek alphabet; and made them pleasantly surprise us by coming up with the second letter, for the first time since 1909.

The new Lancia Beta when it appeared in Turin looked a bit of a mixed bag at first sight. The Fiat engine, across the frame, and with minor differences, did not seem remarkable. Front wheel drive had become a commonplace, and the appearance looked Toyota from the front and Citroen from behind. The inside, especially of the more luxurious models, looked good. The surprise came when people got it on the road, for it was every inch a Lancia in feel, quality, and all those indefinable things which the journalistic jonahs had been convinced were now buried with Vincenzo Lancia. Not so, whatever Giovanni Agnelli, and his Fiat board, had felt they had to do to put the company back on its feet, the preservation of the Lancia image was clearly uppermost in their minds; and it is not much short of a snide remark to say that Lancia is now the up-market Fiat — when was it not?

Hard on the heels of the new saloon came a Coupé and then the HPE, owing a good deal to Tom Karen and the Scimitar idea, it nevertheless worked. And then the mid-engined Monte-Carlo, thought of by most people as the obvious replacement for the little Fulvia Coupé which was still the mainstay of the Rally department, it turned out not to be; for there was yet another surprise on the way.

The Stratos really began its life as a different car altogether, on the Bertone stand at the Turin Show in 1970. At that time it was not a great deal more than a coachbuilders "dream car" using the Fulvia FWD transaxle package mounted amidships and driving the rear wheels. It was the kind of dream that might well become reality. It did; but not in the original guise, for now that the Fiat interests extended not only to Lancia but also to Ferrari, it was possible for Piero Gobbato to negotiate the use of the Dino engine. Of course the Lancia/Ferrari relationship was not new, since the Grand Prix cars had gone to the Commendatore when Lancia wanted to withdraw. What was new was the association with Bertone, as opposed to Farina; but as with Zagato the Lancia mind seems ever open. It was in fact the first time Bertone had been involved in the production of the frame of a car, but they got down to it and the flame-red Stratos was on the stand for the '71 show with the then universal Lancia "HF" on the side.

A year later they got down to testing it, and the rear suspension was immediately changed from double wishbones to MacPherson struts and so it went into business — just how successfully is detailed in the appropriate chapter; but it was a new chapter for Lancia and another step in a remarkable revival.

And now we have the Gamma and a return to that oldest of friendships with Pininfarina. A return too, to the "boxer", or horizontally opposed, four; first mooted for the company in the Flavia by Dr. Fessia some fifteen years before. This is up-market indeed, and in open competition with some of the most notable European cars of the decade. As this goes to press there has scarce been time to assess its qualities; but as the latest in a long line of very lovely ladies, we shall not be far out if we permit ourselves a final flourish, a grace note if you like, which sums up this and so many other Lancias. Popes famous lines:

> *I know a thing that's most uncommon;*
> *(Envy, be silent, and attend!)*
> *I know a reasonable woman,*
> *Handsome and witty, yet a friend.*

BETA

*The first Lancia after the Fiat
Merger, was at great pains to show
that the old touch had not been lost
particularly in the elegant interior.*

From outside the car was not much more than fashionable but was soon to be tidied up.

The HPE (High Performance Estate) was a back-handed compliment to Tom Karen and the Reliant Scimitar, but very well done.

Just how well becomes more apparent when seen in day to day surroundings.

This double spread is devoted to the Monte Carlo, a mid-engined variant, created by Pinin Farina, which has a neatly opening roof as an optional extra.

But to confuse matters, this car with slight amendments is named the Scorpion on the American market. For the record, photographs 1 and 4 are of the American derivative.

BMW *as well as* Reliant *proved a source of inspiration as in this* "Open up but Stay Safe" *coupé.*

The line up shows what standardization can do and below, the Beta coupé — one of the prettiest variants.

STRATOS

The Ferrari engined Stratos started life as a Bertone dream — but one that came true revitalising the firm's image at the same time.

GAMMA

Latest is the Gamma. Up-Market it puts Lancia back where it was in the Astura days — and not before time their friends would say.

And there can be no better friend than Pinin Farina — a Lancia partner from the start, who has once again done them proud.

The fine handsome coupé in which the
Lancia tradition is well maintained
or even enhanced.

CHAPTER EIGHT

Racing and Rallies

Lancia racing, of course, begins with Vicenzo himself, some time before he had formed his own company and when he was working for Fiat. When he did set up on his own, he made a few sporadic appearances in comparatively minor events, and then withdrew altogether. It was some while after his death, that his son Gianni took the firm itself back into racing; and the financial burdens of that decision cost him the company. Later still, under Cesare Fiorio, the company at last made a great success in the world of Rallies. Looked at overall, racing had more sadness in it than pleasure as far as the Lancia family were concerned.

Vincenzo himself was an amiable and persistent driver rather than a world champion — a Chris Amon rather than a Fangio as the record shows. Leaving aside private bets, local speed trials and the like, we have a retirement in the Paris-Madrid, eighth in the 1904 Gordon Bennett; but a win in the Florio Cup. He dropped out of the last Gordon Bennett in 1905, but was third in the Florio and fourth in the Vanderbuilt Cup of the same year. 1907 saw him second in the Targa Florio and sixth in the Kaiserpreis — and so it goes on.

In the end he seemed to drop out of racing without any real regret; and after some luke warm efforts in small events racing ceased to have any part in Lancia's policy.

The whole situation changed in the early fifties when after the introduction of the Aurelia, Gianni Lancia, then in charge of the firm, held a different and perhaps a young man's view. Unlike his father, he determined to put the company into racing, and despite a struggle with some of the directors he got his way. They started with near standard cars; but after an initial success went into sports car racing in a big way with specially built models. The Mille Miglia, Le Mans and finally the Carrera Panamerica became their hunting grounds; and in 1954 they were second in the world sports car championship.

Before that, however, Gianni Lancia had instructed Jano to produce a Grand Prix car; and this he did — showing that he had lost none of his touch during the many intervening years since he had first designed the Monoposto Alfa. The cars had hardly got into their stride when, at Monaco, Ascari put one in the harbour. A week or two later at Monza he was killed in an accident while practicing. The team was disbanded and handed over to Ferrari. The cost had been more than even that unhappy event; for the firm was nearly bankrupt, and the family lost control. The racing programme stopped.

A new lease of competition life came with the Fulvia Coupé; and the appointment of Cesare Fiorio as team manager. Three world championships ending in 1975 have more than established Lancia superiority. The Safari seems to have escaped them, and the new Stratos has produced a rather "horses for courses" situation. But after a lifetime of more downs than ups, they have ended at the top of the heap, at least on the road — and as an advertisement for their product that probably suits them better than any other kind of victory.

A rare photograph of Vincenzo Lancia at the wheel of one of his own cars. Almost all his racing was done for Fiat. The picture was taken on May 5th 1910.

The same year. Lancias appeared amid the dust and smoke in the American Grand Prix.

Paris — St. Petersburg? "Sir! my Lancia driver has been struck by lightening".

Lancia's limited competition effort with the Lambda has left us only one or two nostalgic shots. Above, before the start of the 1925 Gran Premio Turismo at San Sebastian and below in the 1926 "Routes Paviers".

Beggars Roost in the mid thirties.

Many years later the little Aprilia appeared in the Mille Miglia — this is 1951.

By 1952 the B20 Aurelia was being seen as the basis of a fine competition car. Here is a very standard model in the '52 Targa Florio.

*Chiron in the '53 "Monte" — no the passenger is not expressing an opinion of the officials —
rallying was all fun in those far off days.*
*Another Aurelia on the Col de Braus, presumably in the regularity test hence "identifying"
paint slapped on the front.*

Le Havre 1953. The Lancias leave for Mexico attended by their faithful mechanics.

Fangio at full chat during the somewhat blurred proceedings.

And the end of the '53 Carrera Panamerican which Fangio won for Lancias.

Lancia's racing programme in full and successful swing. Above, Taruffi in the '53 Targa Florio and below, an unknown driver in unknown circumstances. Lancia's archives says Taruffi, Automobile Quarterly says Castellotti. "You pays yer penny. . . ."

Chiron in the '54 "Monte" which he won after a magical (almost too good to be true) performance on the regularity tests.

And nothing could be more regular from a Lancia standpoint than the start of the 1954 Coppa 6 ore.

Aurelias (in blue and yellow) at the start of the '54 Mille Miglia. The race numbers denote the starting time.

But they also ran 'real' Sports cars, here is Ascari the eventual winner about to pass a Fiat on the Futa

The Grand Prix of Oporto in '54 saw Villoresi first and Castellotti second. This is Villoresi.

And here is Ascari in the '54 Giro di Sicilia — but did Ascari ever wear a hat like that?

*Cause and effect. Gianni Lancia sits
on the grass at Reims with Alberto
Ascari watching the "Mercs" go
by before asking Jano to design
him a Grand Prix car. Out of
this dream Ascari died and Lancia
lost control of his family's company.*

Luigi Villoresi looks at
Basadonna's shoulder during the 1958
Monte — four years after Chiron had
won the event in a similar car.

A private entrant in the Rally dei
Colli Euganei (1961) and again,
with a different model, in the Rally
delle Dolomiti.

A large and rather standard-looking saloon arrives at Monte Carlo in the '62 event.

Not actually competing, save for advertising honours, the course car at Spain '62.

Far too many of the best pictures turn out to be only the Mobil economy run. Above, an Aurelia in 1962 — and below a Flaminia Coupé in the same event — Incidentally this is the Futa Pass so its not quite such a 'doddle' as you might imagine.

Monte again — a pleasant memory of the end-of-rally round the houses which often resulted in a lot of bent trims but the Lancia looks stable enough as it passes the Casino.

Above, Maglioli's car at Spa. (One of the Zagato models) and on the left, an unknown dicer in the 30th Coppa Gallenga.

The *1965 Coupe de Alpes. All the caption says is "Michèle Mouton."* (*Might as well be hung for a lamb as a goat*).

Lancias in echelon at the end of an Acropolis (*1965*). Remember those funny lights we used to have in the roof?

The 1966 Acropolis. Anderson was first in the 1300 G.T. class and fourth overall and the little coupé was already famous.

Munari and Harris (coming up to St. Auluin) in the 1967 Monte.

Mastermind of Lancia's recent victories is Cesare Fiorio seen here at Sebring in 1967
(dark shirt and cameras behind the car).
Aaltonen talking on the right; and Liddon apparently squashing flies in the roof on the left.
East African Safari 1969.

Munari and Mannucci in the 1972
Monte. On the left the St. Aulnin
special stage and below with a
satisfactory collection of pots after
winning. Lancias were also fourth
and sixth.

The *1972 San Remo, Barlusio and
Sodano — not all the snow is on
the 'Monte'.
Stratos on the Tour de Corse
1972 and a new era opens.*

As much at home in races as in rallies here is Munari in 1973 Targa Florio — he and Andruet were second. Below, a year later, the picture is the same. (Note the radio equipment.)

Munari/Mannucci again in the 1974
San Remo. And on the left Balestieri
with one of the old cars in the
1974 Chamonix 24 hour.

Below, the Lombard Stratos in the
1974 R.A.C.

1975 Monte with those two Ms again and below Waldegard and Thorzelius in Sweden with some rather fancy wheels to help with the snow.

M and M again in the 1975 San Remo with the Stratos and below Sodano in the same event with a Beta coupé (quite a lump by comparison).

Munari and (wait for it!) Meiger in the 1976 Monte.

Munari again in the '76 Safari

And a suitably Safari tailpeice — even though it has never been a "Lancia" event.

Appendix

Lancia Production Car Specifications

Year	Type	Type No.	No. of Cylinders	Bore/Stroke	C.C.	BHP/RPM	Track F/R in mm	Wheelbase in mm	Max.Speed Km/H
1908	Alpha	51	4	90/100	2543	53/1800	1330/1330	2820	90
1908	Dialpha	53	6	90/100	3815	—	1330/1330	3235	110
1909	Beta	54	4	95/110	3120	—	1330/1330	2932	90
1910	Gamma	55	4	100/110	3460	—	1330/1330	2932	110
1911	Delta	56	4	100/130	4080	—	1330/1330	2932	115
1911	Epsilon	58	4	100/130	4080	—	1330/1330	3227	115
1911	Eta	60	4	100/160	5030	—	1330/1330	2775	120
1913	Theta	61	4	110/130	4940	70/2200	1330/1330	3378	120
1919	Kappa	64	4	110/130	4940	70/2200	1330/1330	3388	125
1921	Dikappa	66	4	110/130	4940	87/2300	1365/1370	3388	130
1922	Trikappa	68	8	75/130	4594	98/2500	1365/1370	3384	130
1923	Lambda 214	67	4	75/120	2120	49/3250	1330/1360 1400/1432	3100	115
1925	Lambda 216	67	4	75/120	2120	49/3250	1400/1432	3420	115
1926	Lambda 216 bis	78	4	79/120	2370	59/3250	1400/1432	3420	115
1927	Lambda 218	78	4	79/120	2370	59/3250	1400/1432	3100	115
1928	Lambda 223	79	4	83/120	2570	69/3500	1400/1432	3100	120
1928	Lambda 224	79	4	83/120	2570	69/3500	1400/1432	3420	120
1928	Dilambda 227	81	8	79/100	3960	100/3800	1463/1480	3475	120
1930	Lambda 221A	79	4	83/120	2570	69/3500	1400/1432	3100	125

Year	Type	Type No.	No. of Cylinders	Bore Stroke	C.C.	BHP/ RPM	Track F/R in mm	Wheelbase in mm	Max. Speed Km/H
1930	Lambda 222A	79	4	83/120	2570	69/3500	1400/1432	3420	125
1930	Dilambda 229	81A	8	79/100	3960	100/3800	1424/1442	3290	130
1931	Astura 230	85	8	70/85	2604	73/4000	1374/1396	3177	125
1931	Artena 228	84	4	83/90	1925	55/4000	1374/1396	2990	115
1932	Dilambda 232	81A	8	79/100	3960	100/3800	1424/1442	3475	120
1933	Augusta 231	88	4	70/78	1196	35/4000	1196/1210 1210/1223	2650	102
1934	Astura 233-233C	91	8	75/85	2972	82/4000	1374/1396	3332 3100	130
1934	Artena 228A & C	84	4	83/90	1925	55/4000	1374/1396	3180 2950	110
1937	Aprilia 238	97	4	72/83	1352	48/4300	1236/1266 1262/1292	2750	126
1939	Aprilia 438	99	4	75/85	1486	48/4300	1262/1292	2750	126
1939	Aprilia 439	99	4	75/85	1486	48/4300	1262/1292	2850	113
1939	Ardea 250	100-100A	4	65/68	903	29/4600	1162/1180	2440	108
1946	Aprilia 539, 539/2	99	4	75/85	1486	48/4300	1262/1318	2950	116
1948	Ardea 3rd Series 250	100A	4	65/68	903	29/4600	1162/1180	2440	108
1949	Ardea 4th Series 250	100B	4	65/68	903	30/4600	1162/1180	2440	108
1950	Aurelia B10	B10	6	70/76	1754	57/4700	1280/1300	2860	135
1951	Aurelia B21, B21S	B21	6	72/82	1991	70/4800	1280/1300	2860	145
1951	Aurelia G.T. B20	B20	6	72/82	1991	80/5000	1280/1300	2660	162
1952	Aurelia B15, B15S	B15	6	72/82	1991	64/4800	1300/1320	3250	133
1952	Aurelia B22, B22S	B22	6	72/82	1991	90/5000	1280/1300	2860	160
1953	Aurelia G.T. 2500, B20	B20	6	78/86	2451	116/5200	1280/1300	2660	185
1953	Appia C10, C10S	C10	4	68/75	1090	38/4800	1178/1182	2480	120

Year	Type	Type No.	No. of Cylinders	Bore Stroke	C.C.	BHP/RPM	Track F/R in mm	Wheelbase in mm	Max. Speed Km/H
1954	Aurelia 2nd Series B12, B12S	B12	6	75/86	2266	85/4800	1280/1300	2850	151
1955	Aurelia Spider B24, B24S	B24	6	78/86	2451	116/5000	1290/1300	2450	180
1956	Appia 2nd Series C10, C10S	C10	4	68/75	1090	44/4800	1178/1182	2510	128
1956	Aurelia G.T. 2500 B20, B20S	B20	6	78/86	2451	110/5300	1280/1300	2650	176
1956	Aurelia Convertible B24S	B24	6	78/86	2451	110/5300	1280/1300	2450	172
1957	Aurelia G.T. 2500 B20, B20S	B20	6	78/86	2451	112/5300	1280/1300	2650	180
1957	Aurelia Convertible B24S	B24	6	78/86	2451	112/5300	1280/1300	2450	175
1957	Flaminia 813.00	813.00	6	80/82	2458	100/4800	1368/1370	2870	160
1959	Appia 3S, 808.07, 808.08	808.07	4	68/75	1090	48/5200	1180/1182	2510	132
1959	Flaminia Coupé P. Farina	823.00	6	80/82	2458	119/5600	1368/1370	2750	170
1959	Flaminia G.T. Touring	823.00	6	80/82	2458	119/5600	1368/1370	2520	180
1959	Flaminia Sport Zagato	823.00	6	80/82	2458	119/5600	1368/1370	2520	190
1960	Flaminia Cnv. G.T. Touring	823.00	6	80/82	2458	119/5600	1368/1370	2520	178
1960	Flavia 815.00	815.00	4	82/71	1500	78/5400	1300/1280	2650	148
1960	Appia 3S Giardinetta 808.21	808.07	4	68/75	1090	48/5200	1180/1182	2510	120
1961	Appia Sport 812.05	814.00	4	68/75	1090	60/5400	1180/1182	2350	160
1961	Flaminia 813.10, 813.11	813.10	6	80/82	2458	110/5200	1368/1370	2870	167
1961	Flaminia G.T. 824.10	823.10	6	80/82	2458	140/5600	1368/1370	2520	191
1961	Flaminia Sport 824.13	823.10	6	80/82	2458	140/5600	1368/1370	2520	200
1961	Flaminia Convertible 824.14	823.10	6	80/82	2458	140/5600	1368/1370	2520	190
1962	Flaminia Speciale 813.12	823.10	6	80/82	2458	140/5600	1368/1370	2870	180
1962	Flavia Coupé 815.130	815.100	4	82/71	1500	90/5800	1300/1280	2480	171

Year	Type	Type No.	No. of Cylinders	Bore Stroke	C.C.	BHP/ RPM	Track F/R in mm	Wheelbase in mm	Max. Speed Km/H
1962	Flaminia Coupé 823.02	823.00	6	80/82	2458	128/5600	1368/1370	2750	178
1962	Flavia Convertible 815.134	815.100	4	82/71	1500	90/5800	1300/1280	2480	171
1963	Fulvia 818.00	818.00	4	72/67	1091	58/6000	1300/1280	2480	138
1963	Flavia 1.8, 815.300	815.300	4	88/74	1800	86/5500	1300/1280	2650	160
1963	Flavia Coupé 1.8, 815.330	815.300	4	88/74	1800	88/5650	1300/1280	2480	173
1963	Flavia Conv. 1.8, 815.334	815.300	4	88/74	1800	88/5650	1300/1280	2480	173
1963	Flavia Sport 1.3, 815.532	815.500	4	88/74	1800	95/6000	1300/1280	2480	180
1963	Flaminia 2.8, 826.000	826.000	6	85/82	2775	125/5300	1368/1370	2870	170
1963	Flaminia Coupé 2.8, 826.030	826.030	6	85/82	2775	136/5450	1368/1370	2750	181
1963	Flaminia Sport 2.8, 826.132	826.100	6	85/82	2775	146/5600	1368/1370	2520	200
1963	Flaminia Conv. 2.8, 826.134	826.100	6	85/82	2775	146/5600	1368/1370	2520	193
1963	Flaminia G.T. 2.8, 826.138	826.100	6	85/82	2775	146/5600	1368/1370	2520	194
1963	Flaminia G.T.L. 2.8, 826.140	826.100	6	85/82	2775	146/5600	1368/1370	2600	191
1963	Flavia 815.200	815.200	4	80/74	1488	75/5600	1300/1280	2650	150
1964	Fulvia 2C, 818.100	818.100	4	72/67	1091	71/6200	1300/1280	2480	145
1964	Flaminia Super Sport 826.232	826.200	6	85/82	2775	148/5900	1368/1370	2520	210
1965	Fulvia Coupé 818.130	818.130	4	76/67	1216	80/6200	1300/1280	2330	160
1965	Flavia Berlina 815.400	815.400	4	88/74	1800	102/5800	1300/1280	2650	168
1965	Flavia Coupé 815.430	815.400	4	88/74	1800	102/5800	1300/1280	2480	180
1965	Flavia Sport 815.432	815.400	4	88/74	1800	102/5800	1300/1280	2480	188
1965	Flavia Convertible 815.434	815.400	4	88/74	1800	102/5800	1300/1280	2480	180
1965	Fulvia Sport 818.-32	818.132	4	76/67	1216	80/6200	1300/1280	2330	169

Year	Type	Type No.	No. of Cylinders	Bore Stroke	C.C.	BHP/ RPM	Track F/R in mm	Wheelbase in mm	Max. Speed Km/H
1966	Fulvia Coupé H.F. 818.140	818.140	4	76/67	1216	88/6200	1300/1280	2330	161
1967	Fulvia G.T. 818.200	818.130	4	76/67	1216	80/6200	1300/1280	2480	152
1967	Fulvia Coupé 1.3, 818.330	818.302	4	77/70	1298	87/6200	1300/1280	2330	168
1967	Fulvia Sport 1.3, 818.332	818.302	4	77/70	1298	87/6200	1300/1280	2330	176
1967	Fulvia Coupé 1.3 H.F. 818.340	818.342	4	77/70	1298	101/6500	1300/1280	2330	174
1967	Fulvia G.T. 818.200	818.202	4	75/70	1231	80/6200	1300/1280	2480	152
1967	Fulvia Coupé 818.130	818.202	4	75/70	1231	80/6200	1300/1280	2330	160
1967	Flavia 819.200	819.200	4	80/74	1488	80/5600	1320/1280	2650	152
1967	Flavia 819.300	819.300	4	88/74	1800	92/5700	1320/1280	2650	165
1967	Flavia 819.400	819.400	4	88/74	1800	102/5800	1320/1280	2650	170
1968	Fulvia G.T.E. 818.300	818.302	4	77/70	1298	87/6200	1300/1280	2480	161
1968	Fulvia Coupé S 818.360	818.303	4	77/70	1298	103/6200	1300/1280	2330	173
1968	Fulvia 818.282, 818.292	818.282	4	74/70	1199	87/6200	1300/1280	2480	152
1968	Fulvia Sport 818.362	818.303	4	77/70	1298	103/6200	1300/1280	2330	180
1969	Flavia 819.200	819.202	4	77/80	1490	84/5600	1320/1280	2650	152
1969	Flavia 819.300	819.302	4	85/80	1815	96/5700	1320/1280	2650	165
1969	Flavia Coupé 820.030	820.000	4	89/80	1991	131/5800	1320/1280	2480	185
1969	Flavia 2000, 819.610	820.000	4	89/80	1991	131/5800	1320/1280	2650	175
1969	Fulvia Coupé 1.6, 818.540	818.540	4	82/75	1584	130/6500	1390/1335	2330	180
1969	Fulvia 2nd Series 818.610	818.302	4	77/70	1298	95/6200	1300/1280	2500	161
1969	Flavia Coupé 820.430	820.400	4	89/80	1991	140/5800	1320/1280	2480	190
1969	Flavia 2000, 819.810	820.400	4	89/80	1991	140/5800	1320/1280	2650	180

Year	Type	Type No.	No. of Cylinders	Bore Stroke	C.C.	BHP/RPM	Track F/R in mm	Wheelbase in mm	Max. Speed Km/H
1969	Fulvia 2nd Series 818.692	818.282	4	74/70	1199	87/6200	1300/1280	2500	152
1970	Fulvia Coupé 818.630	818.303	4	77/70	1298	90/6200	1300/1280	2330	170
1970	Fulvia Sport 818.650	818.303	4	77/70	1298	90/6200	1300/1280	2330	180
1970	Fulvia Coupé H.F. 818.740	818.540	4	82/75	1584	114/6500	1390/1335	2330	180
1970	Fulvia 2nd Series 818.612	818.302	4	77/70	1298	85/6200	1300/1280	2500	160
1970	Fulvia 2nd Series 818.694	818.282	4	74/70	1199	78/6200	1300/1280	2500	152
1971	Flavia 2000, 820.010	820.000	4	89/80	1991	114/5800	1320/1280	2650	175
1971	Flavia 2000 I, 820.410	820.400	4	89/80	1991	131/5800	1320/1280	2650	180
1971	Lancia 2000, 820.210	820.200	4	89/80	1991	115/6000	1320/1280	2650	175
1971	Lancia Coupé 2000, 820.230	820.200	4	89/80	1991	115/6000	1332/1288	2480	185
1971	Fulvia Sport 1600, 818.750	818.540	4	82/75	1584	114/6500	1300/1280	2330	190
1971	Lancia Coupé H.F. 820.436	820.406	4	89/80	1991	125/6000	1332/1288	2480	190
1972	Lancia 2000, 820.210	820.200	4	89/80	1991	115/6000	1332/1288	2650	175
1972	Lancia 2000 I.E. 820.416	820.406	4	89/80	1991	125/6000	1332/1288	2650	180
1972	Fulvia Coupé 1.3 Monte Carlo 813.630	818.303	4	77/70	1298	90/6200	1300/1280	2330	170
1972	Beta 1600, 828. AB.0	828 A	4	80/79	1592	100/6400	1406/1392	2540	170
1972	Beta 1800, 828 AB.1	828 A1.	4	84/79	1756	110/6400	1406/1392	2540	175
1973	Beta 1400, 828 AB.2	828 A2.	4	80/72	1438	90/6400	1406/1392	2540	165
1974	Beta 1600, 828 AC.0	828 AC.0	4	80/79	1592	106/6400	1406/1392	2350	180
1974	Beta 1800, 828 AC.1	828 AC.1	4	84/79	1756	120/6400	1406/1392	2350	190
1974	Stratos 829 AR.c	829 A	6	93/60	2418	190/7800	1430/1460	2180	230

Year	Type	Type No.	No. of Cylinders	Bore Stroke	C.C.	BHP/RPM	Track F/R in mm	Wheelbase in mm	Max. Speed Km/H
1974	Beta Spider 828 AS.0	828 AC.0	4	80/79	1592	106/6400	1406/1392	2350	178
1974	Beta Spider 828 AS.1	828 AC.1.	4	84/79	1756	120/6400	1406/1392	2350	186
1975	Beta 1300, 828 BB3.A	828 B3	4	76/72	1297	82/6400	1406/1392	2540	160
1975	H.P.E. 1600, 828 A.F.0	828 A	4	84/72	1585	100/6400	1406/1392	2540	174
1975	H.P.E. 1800, 828 AF.1.	828 A1	4	84/90	1995	119/6400	1406/1392	2540	180
1975	Beta 1600, 828 CB.0	828 B	4	84/72	1585	100/6400	1406/1392	2540	170
1975	Beta 2000, 828 CB.1.	828 B1	4	84/90	1995	119/6400	1406/1392	2540	180
1975	Beta 1300, 828 CB3.A	828 B3	4	76/72	1297	82/6400	1406/1392	2540	160
1975	Beta 1600, 828 BC.0	828 B	4	84/72	1585	100/6400	1406/1392	2350	178
1975	Beta 2000, 828 BC.1.	828 B1	4	84/90	1995	119/6400	1406/1392	2350	188
1975	Beta Spider 828 BS.0	828 B	4	84/72	1585	100/6400	1406/1392	2350	176
1975	Beta Spider 828 BS.1.	828 B1	4	84/90	1995	119/6400	1406/1392	2350	186
1975	H.P.E. 1600, 828 BF.0	828 B	4	84/72	1585	100/6400	1406/1392	2540	174
1975	H.P.E. 2000, 828 BF.1	828 BF.1	4	84/90	1995	119/6400	1406/1392	2540	180
1975	Beta Monte Carlo 137 AS.	137 AS.	4	84/90	1995	120/6000	1412/1456	2300	190

Some of the motor cars
exhibited at the
Vincenzo Lancia Museum
in Turin

ALPHA

BETA

THETA

LAMBDA

DILAMBDA

ARTENA